HAPPINESS

HAPPINESS
MARTIN HARRISON

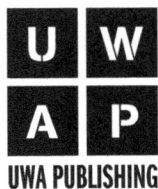

UWA PUBLISHING

First published in 2015 by
UWA Publishing
Crawley, Western Australia 6009
www.uwap.uwa.edu.au

UWAP is an imprint of UWA Publishing
a division of The University of Western Australia

THE UNIVERSITY OF
WESTERN
AUSTRALIA

National Library of Australia Cataloguing-in-Publication entry:
Harrison, Martin, 1949–2014 author.
Happiness / Martin Harrison.
ISBN: 9781742586861 (paperback)
Australian poetry.
A821.3

Typeset in Bembo by Lasertype
Printed by Lightning Source

This project has been assisted by the Australian Government
through the Australia Council, its arts funding and advisory body.

Australian Government

Australia
Council
for the Arts

ACKNOWLEDGEMENTS AND PUBLICATION DETAILS

I would like to thank the Literature Board of the Australia Council for a residency at the Keesing Studio in Paris in 2008. Thanks also to Michael Brennan in one of whose Rare Object chapbooks, *Living Things*, a handful of the poems were collected in 2013. The book, as a whole offering, is for the late Nizar Bouheni (1984–2010).

Introduction

.

Martin Harrison (1949–2014) was a poet, essayist and teacher. He absorbed and responded to many currents in twentieth century poetry, the Cambridge Poets, the Spanish Modernistas and a strand of environmental encounter powerful in recent Australian poetry. His intellectual range was broad, far-reaching but brilliantly coherent: his essays were invariably passionate and measured conversations in which cultures, situations and artists found themselves subtly enhanced, deepened – their place in our fate made more serious. His teaching, like his writing, was an art of active listening. He would have agreed with Jorge-Luis Borges when he wrote, 'I have not taught the love of particular texts; I have taught my students how to love literature, how to see literature as a form of happiness.' The feeling for form supported the connection he made between communing and community. His attention to the distribution of voices expressed a desire of absorption: the epiphanic solitudes that typify his greatest poems describe moments when he assumes the flesh of the world. In his doctoral thesis, 'On Composition', Harrison wrote, 'The cognitive definition of writing, which is to say a writing caught in the process of formation as a writing prone to error and repeat and redaction from multiple versions, is ultimately crossed out, if for no other good reason than this: what turns out to be a more permanent version, for example a later draft, supersedes an earlier transitory version. Even if we imagine a version where errors are let stay and read whether as scribbled mistakes or emendations added to the text, even these crossings-out become fixed textual evidences.' The poems of *Happiness* translate this insight into experiments with punctuation, with voice – with, in short, composition. Multilayered micro-narratives documenting a dive into the time of desire supplement those histories of arrest and sensuous exfoliation, which are Harrison's unique and abiding subject. In these poems time is also broken off. *Happiness* was being prepared for publication in the month of his death, September 2014. Martin Harrison's *Wild Bees: New and Selected Poems* was published by University of Western Australia Publishing, first appearing in 2008. *Happiness* selects from his poetry since then.

Paul Carter, May 2015

CONTENTS

Happiness

White Flowers

The air the wind the outside and outsize
of what's possible and imaginable
clear and clean endeavour into the atmosphere
of light on dark and glittering spaces
where crimson rosellas swerve sideways
into cascades of down-hanging white flowers
they land whistling in that snowy down
that galactic spray of weeping branches
now revealing themselves in an entirety
of whitenesses for a few days in a
suddenness which takes my breath away
because the enormity of the thousands
of pale-yellow-hearted four-petaled flowerlets
is an act of exposure on so huge a scale –
and to what? the wind, the next moon,
the rain-streaked winter light? the sun? –
and because the suddenness is
what suddenly and surreptitiously
strikes you (invisible, unthought
awareness) as the same naked revealedness
of your lover beneath you, beside
you or above you caught there
where humanness itself is flowering light
ecstatic with joy in the act of love

Poems

Wallabies

…some memories from somewhere those scattered trees
that straggle of white tree limbs like bleached bones

perhaps a line from someone else or myself
memory of the flattest waters I've ever seen

emerging dreamlike from the low brown skyline
bouquets of white cockatoos bursting from the leaves

out-of-time movement over the dead stubble
what've they been doing? they've been hiding

they've been hiding in the mind, in the body
and then some images of suddenly meeting

that low brown water's thin mirror
as if the crowd of trees signalled to it, or had been

signalling all their lives, building riverine clusters,
building their wandering cicatrice seen from far off –

but when you get there it's the necessary damage
of banks and flooded logs, dried up pools, Toyota paths

nestled spots to fish from the ones safe to swim
flickering shadows hands of them sweeping over the sand

that sense too of clayed ground of earth dust grit pebbles
shards of bark crumbling the crumble and dust of leaves

earth hard with veins of muddy tree roots showing there
wooden dark veins jutting through aged flesh

everywhere the scatter of light from the ground upwards
brilliance of dry dead things shining back in your face

great uplifted spaces glistening with blueness warm air
scent of honeyed fragrant pollens and of less sweet wax

heat smell like some soft linen's invisible cushion
the light threads of native bees, chases of flies

cicadas clicking and humming their electric shavers a
sound system hiddenly installed inside the halfway

bare dancefloor over there between the bottlebrushes
their sawing rhythm nearly as toneless as wooden clacks

but it picks up like an outboard then dies to comes back
saw-toothed that side not noticed now this side here

the great long wave of cicadas breaking like fire
night's burnt firemarks streaked down tree-boles' white flesh:

afternoon's white flesh is the memory of this
the thing which is hidden like a name is hidden

an island which is islanded because it is so far away
because it floats between skylines where distant grey trees

hover above the ground where things appear as if
in appearance they've acted on you they live they breathe

nothing is dead here the spaces between them are
inhabited leaves twigs debris fallen white-anted trunks

slopes rocks grass parrots galahs floating down
in pink streamers again the grey lack of edge

around sprays cream waterfalls of turpentines flowering
in high irrigated air-blue reaches she-oaks aspirant

with their million fingers and amber seed-flowers
spotted gums mottled as grandmothers but with contrasts

of grey brown white and silver as if dressed for a ball
the reds of the king parrot slashing the foliage

with its opening and closing flower as it flies up
vertically to land yes a blinding red and blue male

these flashes of thought these memories now planted
these hard-cased seeds needing fire to sprout these nets

of dirt leaf and twig where ants fossick mason bees sandmine
these laceworks of bark litter and dropped branches

are inland floodwater you wade through to get to land
they're the fuel for the long sweep of the mind's eye

a blanket building up over the worst sterility and death
radiance offers sore bruises earth turns to clay and bakes

an imaginary tide holds blood and featherdown in flight
in place on the edge in the middle in the heart's moment

in the absent space between regions rapidly turned blue
as the ridges stretching west the gulleys sharp as razors

echo after echo after echo of a sound tracking in peaks
till it scratches small shimmers on rocks smoothed by wind

then it lays its long body out there called the west
it's the land scarcely touching the earth swarms of them

it's the land dotted with saltbrush and bush tomato
that twenty mile shadow across the claypan's a fence

which as dusk comes is a lightning-quick snake
momentarily distracting the way they appear

as if from nowhere like sentinels weathered stone
camping in that stubble sunset-toned no like mushrooms

wallabies two of them and then three over there then more
pale half-red underfur letting them melt into late light

alert as the slanting hour's alert to earth cool as wine
then the shriek as they scatter having nursed the air

having known everything as the waking dreamer
knows everything for a scattered instant instantly gone

time's far-sighted body felt beloved and lost in time
the memory of it like the memory of a lover

as familiar as a body curled around yours each day
just like when evaporating inland daybreak starts you wake

"In the air's touch, round..."

In the air's touch, round
our bodies intertwined   touch, gaze
there's the desire which brings us not just longed-for presence
but definition each to the other in touch and gaze renewed
that play which asks how far the face the lips the arms the inclined
body held explored crotch and cock
can go   all in the same breath as we can feel
the border which we imagine between lucid water luscious sand
together with a new vowelled, strict vocabulary drawn from air
wordless movement in the tender ledge of movement
the wind-smoked wave forming behind the wave in the wave
of which, later, we most likely half-think something exotic like

dusk's orange-breasted swallow circling the white minaret

Poem

Even for a moment to forget you – that can only be pain
(the dilution, distilled sunlight, cracked cement by an entrance)

Each day we risk such loss, unfixable loss
(the slow dissolve, daybreak light on clouds like broccoli leaves)

The clock-hand's motion a dream in which there's no movement
(the ute turns the corner, pulls over on a gravel verge by the bridge)

The time is all time and the no-time left is like spent breath
(once again that honey-eater glances through space like a green dart)

Each poem about you is the oldest ever, repeating truest nonsense
(I desire you, you make love to me, rain-storms glitter in channels)

Patio

At any moment
any slice or gash,
a huge explosion falling
in any direction –

outside the window
a swatch of bladed leaves
sways this way that way
inside the frame:

wordless day bounces
down the tree's bare limbs,
through its outspread flamboyance
toward twigs and wattle-birds

while they maraud sticky cream flowers
as if beauty could be instantly
sucked from the world.
Directly. Without irony.

A Glance

1. Evening At Home

Rain means darkness,
glitter on a cloud edge
meeting the air
where it cascades to ice. −

Rain means darkness
meeting the air. Falling,
each shower wants to be
its own shelter,
to curl over
like a creature
staying warm in woven
grass, in warm earth
day-dreaming: in fact, rain
would like not to be rain
but to be that sun-struck room,
that dry light space. It would like
not to be moodily drifting
down empty streets
as in some old black-and-white
photo − a town in Belgium
circa 1920s or sidings glimpsed
outside Pittsburgh in the 40s −
but to be just cool in
the sense of chic. That way,
it might offer an anticipation −
an utterly intimate feeling −
of physical well-being
which − after all, being rain − it alone
can offer.
    Do you see this?
The shadow thrown now
across the table,
a night of winter showers

14

streaking the uncurtained
glass window, streaking
its mirror-effect:
it's the other side
of the planet,
it's where I come from
held deeply in mind
as I sit here working
getting information from
the screen – all the time,
I'm thinking of you,
aching for your kiss,
aching to touch you
right now. Don't you see this?

2. Poplars

Warm cool play of sun on poplars trembling
wind-rusted, standing out like torches in olive-green hordes
lines, strings, and flows:
an old stone wall behind them,
tracks snake through dusty grass

—cobbles of water are the colour of dark blue eyes,
sharp light rippling a guitar
then far out a wind running like sheep before ruffling into bright water,
the dodge, the turn, the dash like a football player seeking a break
shimmering depths
hill-slopes dipping to them
everywhere a long hand of still unended summer heat,
the place is brimming as if hot air's blown grit in your eye   or the dust's
swirled up just now along the road

—poplars for a second taller than those other suddenly startled
                                        white sheep
which have poured out behind the range
billowing translucent pillowed bulging tinted grey-white
real clouds yet looking as if photographed
a wall of them cresting sun-bleached hills
pretending a change which will be relayed elsewhere
sent up the inland in tomorrow's muggy electric storm
but here now to bring
an extra sense of tranquil animal seeing (bland, long cow-gazes of clouds!)
faces looming over a fence or a wall

: but what I'm saying is something different
not quite beyond describing
how you look at me   how you look back
how a moment returns every time I look into your eyes
light-filled physical
in which we stare out time's grain

16

the thread the broken weave that's taking us
through memories and future senses
as if we're standing somewhere
looking across blue distances of a
long slope back to mountains and down there a lake
to which we'll drive
and be surprised by poplars (1950s plantings) now drifting down a
                                    few gold leaves
but most of them are still trembling on their branches
in the late season's unusual warm wind

About Bats

The bats which got in
last night
through the broken extractor fan
upstairs
while we were talking
on the phone

tiny micro-bats
with pale chests and
black-brown wings three times their pygmy-shrew
body size: they touch surfaces
in soft, velvet splatters,
they land like dusters,
they're softness (a word hard to stomach in poems),
they make the air flutter when they swerve around,
their speed so fine they look like dark flames
evaporating in mid-space –

well, the bats
were that "soft" surprise moment –
at first I'd thought one of them
then thought two,
letting one out of the window –
really, there'd been three –
whirling in mid-air like shape-shifters
or like genii
like magic hands
in the electric lamplight

that breeze flittering round me
caused by bats, let's call it zephyr
(French ones are "bald mice")
let's call them "gentle-breeze-mice"
as the Chinese might do
acknowledging
the way their webbed paws

"wings"
give a huge circling embrace
to a small part of the world,
fitting in through frequency

guessing contours
sheering away and around
without sight   alert through the whole
system to the looming bulk tanker
twenty storeys tall on the long dark swollen Pacific Ocean
(the refrigerator near the door)
or the fine filigree of currents
(my pedestal fan) in their flight's veer
and dart

objects being sensed in their richness
along every fibre,
in every nerve as possible harshness,
as passage and entry,
as cloths and clouds through the muscle
held forever
as a branch of apple flowers blossoming –
on the edge –
in the river of movements where
air and water meet constantly
a river of sun-flashes sensitised like a dancer's
placing of a physical counterpoint on a rhythm:

bats being themselves makers of shape and shaping
shapers of a purely undefinable intuitive shape
not unlike a gesture of
pure thoughtless good intent
in which each creature
(in mind or urge, it's the same)
(heard or overheard, there's no difference)
changes into the volume and shift

of things fingered out between
thought and love and flesh

: small black bats circling and
soaring in the kitchen at night

Summer Rain Front, North Coast

A summer rain front laces a trailing hat of mist

around the headland's mountain: a saucer of mist

scraping the tree-tops   hanging over rock outcrops

Imagine it whispering through the branches,

caught on the slope

The mountain wears its hat like a Chinese boatman

Only here, only now, this bit of coast could do it –

a suddenness of rain and moisture among the months of drought

with things changing, things coming to an end

and before it, the ocean's clarity

the smooth blue translucent sea emerging in a sun-burst

sky clearing as the blood clears   the mist trails hanging

the rich, green slopes darker than cedars

spindly arms of die-back trees sharp as cotton threads of white,

while longer shadows move imperceptibly

from water into trees

and the mist-hat

taking on a bluer tinge, a sculpted shape

wet summery light etching the thing into

a space more visible, more real, than anything luminously sublime

slipping its shape into the eye beyond the edge of words

better defined than digital TV   knife-like sharp and separated

yet reflected there, merged, blended into water   and so,

to be remembered constantly   to be remembered coastally

as if the mountain and its mist have this propensity

in the production and intenseness of attraction

the mountain mirrored in the instant's stillness

of the calm sea flooding into the bay

the mountain photoing its image on the waters

over the grounds where dolphins track   and then its scarves

hanging high in the air like drifted parachutes

white against blue   grey against blue   edges smudged into the blue such an instance bringing with it delight's suddenness

as if in the guise of bird or angel gathered in the lucid air

What is the mountain doing at the headland

why is it there   thing most "thing" of things shaped upwards

against the sky's wishes even if it is the sky

which bathes each contour

familiar with it over aeons and the presence

of trees, sun, rain and water about which

nothing needs be done   the connections rest

back of the mind, back of time   an event is made

through each and all its shifting lines

a grey-backed gull hovering above the water will soon plunge

far out, a sea-wave's silky whiteness starts to flower, then breaks

The blue-green slope flatters the ocean with its white-ant greys

its fluctuating greens   its underscore of cavernous marine they're *so* close   it's so phenomenal!   the cavernous blue

within the dark of every branch and every depth

in which a necessary shift is richness beyond the eye's ability

to see the thing it loves and love it so again

(what do I see?)   how is there love such as this

proceeding from the heart of things   the brain of things

glimpsed like some familiar sense of air and space

a phrase so familiarly known you don't hear it

or a thought so tantalising loaded in the tissue

a black crow's feathers fluttering   a word tossed out across

the gritty wind of a car park   parallelism of intentions

or just some pure greeting   pure love   The mountain wreathed in last night's

Daybreak

6.30. Startup. Bird twitter,
honey-eaters, blue wrens,

one of last night's mosquitoes
still dancing through new half-light –

a dented, flowing river-light –
split into a moment's diamond

with breeze and leaves,
the house roof, the ridge slope:

the irreversible time,
the birdlike mood

(birdlike because always moving,
perching, quickly alarmed, sharp)

flicker memories of you
hidden into wakefulness

like a facet, see-through,
an unnameable conclusion.

Paris Poems

1. You Do All These Things For Me

Lemon intensity in each muscle same as frail winter light in half-leaved trees
glow which is neither coming nor going   glow in the world beyond the
    world
the one where all this breath is going all these ah's and oh's
breath held there at the limit of breath being the same limit as the moment
when a translucent blue green wave starts to topple
tiny grey fish floating in its upright wall
the top of it bristling with foam and wind-driven sprays of flowers
no more no more more no more
Paris November sunset turning to butter
unsalted pale light seeming to be me to be you
there's no turning back where the gravel path curves through the trees
the gleaming wave flickers through the laurels which can't be excerpted
all the other meanings topple with the sliding uprearing surface
gritty wind in my ears sweaty hair how much faster we must drive
the children's cries left in a playground's far corner
further and further away than anything you've ever invented
dark leaf-strewn copper shadow
who knows what to do
the sudden shift is the light is the time commenced
in the moment which is not language which
cannot be said following the body's hot river
which flows between us your shoulder more rounded than hillsides
and you infolding the world like it's a shape more familiar than air
your body's pressure more firm than earth A frail light is a

2. A Park

in the thicket of it all

ey stretching from west to east and along the edges these mixes of greens
from sempiternal
the creamy lighter green of something with waxen leaves
nameless as peripheral
dreams
when, at the end of long balustrades, they fall
in sprays of ivy and blood-red creeper –
a thick-grown wind-shivered waterfall –
splayed along almost paint-free concrete
near the stairway with its buttress and weathered corbal:
shrivelled red
like hands which are stars in flight down a scrolling
of vines and fruits – sky and misty horizons
have brought into the world this vertical levelling
of leaf-edge, space and stem –
shrivelled crimson like old bruised skin like dust
leaves along the windy terrace blowing
autumn over broken pavers
patches of afternoon sun are like lakes
whose imperceptible edges manoeuvre
time and the ground's weight
opening up exactly what's required
enough space for a year
or a hundred years
– miniature arena of bareness –
– sun-shadows are dancers' footmarks –
over there   just over there   till
like a (flicker) black (light-burst) wing
the sudden cloud-threat of children's voices
arguing, playing, echoing, shouting
under the overhangs and green hollows and shadow arches
/a gravelled carriage-way leading into everybody's far-flung/

how will I have grown in a few years? and such anxiety –
will it ever wither and fall, fall as leaf and mist? It hangs
there in an old upstairs cupboard, dreamt. A half-thought. A thing
like an undisturbed, black bat. The play of greennesses
more swollen in those trees than a sore ankle – ah well you've been running
over the fresh-cut grass, dark stripes left from new mowing,
its fragrance in the soon to be dewed air
its richness, its movement like an old house's drive sweeps round

– *leaves and thoughts in the thick of it*

3. Leaving Paris

Harfleur

The vase in pieces the window in pieces the curtains torn
the map of Australia in pieces
the arrows between here and there drawn on a table
but really in pieces   how does time flow with ease
what's the meaning of marble
The next steps forward are all staircases
I'd have thought the entrance at Harfleur is a breeze
grown-up girls hang out there doing their gavottes
grrrrrrr grrrrrr seagulls
white as alabaster who can fly down south
wing-free no longer prisoners
I'm a prisoner here why can't anyone see it
like a silk rug that someone's shaking a long "collapsed" wave collapses
I'm a rug? he inquires
no it's just a ruined building filled with voices
you can hear them doing their faces   each pitch's a scale
collapsed ruined as he found you
there in the tennis-park which the tempest's wrought
and running by it deeper a gulf of sulphurs
the violin river's playing in my head dark waters light waters
a gull hovering battling the air it's interminable
no less than the part of the present I'm not living in   and which is you
given how you run faster than light into another world
everything you give off moving faster than purest desert light

Half-Flowers

The columns move to the river and sometimes are
rising up like artificial doves   sprays of white flowers
in stone and glass   The cheval gallops on shards
There is no way to hold out against the stone which cannot be ah
ermmmm oh   words end like cauliflowers
words rend like drover tours
final sounds like a lemon will demur   a lemon which makes a pout
even if we have always drunk our tea,   ,   the thought is yours
I came out at the end of the half-leaved alley in a daze
(cough) in a dance the carriage and four out of control
something's cooking lots of little ones the blossoms
perhaps and the river lilies shimmering there in a blaze
like a shelf of unbaked pots the fleshtones of the blaze dulled me
how couldn't we imagine them as children heading off to summer
an experience of vacuum is an experience of
in which entire continents of living reduce to mulled me
osotis millions of flea-sized flowers blue and white
palace windows stare down the partly trimmed hedges
(p.s. I'm indifferent to structures of 12)
palace widows stare over partly trimmed delight
didn't they lose everybody? have we still not got the toll?
in the downdraft of ghosts I just can't get over my guilt
even when language moves closer to the mind
for both of them have different names   neither being soul

Paris

or funk   *aawww*
(message arrives)   one hundred and thirty four samples
there was a time when we could go in a single direction
picking up more and more dust across the *"pampa"* More and more
music brought about the arrival of present time *duhhhh*
like the whole ensemble was a weather pattern more intense
than real rain hitting tin   I've just miked my toe
you last cricked the row   you made it here like a *gangsta*
whose time never arrives in one place uh piece
I mean puce you gotta keep up the place
it's looking more disorganised than a sty
don't you remember when we owned and didn't lease
like a vast expanse the size of Lake Eyre two piccoli whistle
"or func"   "ore" a phone call costs nothing
bread was unreal   ticking time didn't take over like Scottish thistle
I mean plural   A sottish burial is a wondrous thing   like a bustle
      in which there's no time just the same movement and repeat
(an emotional life dies under the impact of these glimpses)
each glimpse is a glimpse on its own   Not even a glance
will do when there're so many bushes to beat
around in the time of those great composers who dreamed stars
awesome stairs and not horseless weirs   *aaaawwwww*
frank fun is the order of the decaying times we live among not in
there's no end to the bits and pieces of our tares and tears

Blackberry

"Let the president have his blackberry"
always two jaws gnawing at the food we've freed
the image resting longer than the mark which feeds it
and the design attributes of Tom and Jerry
the last act is too much seriousness The ferry
leaves in half an hour taking us back to where they came
from (a cloud of horses floats along the street) in Christiana
which is back there in a surry in a slurry of snow and terry
the sepia of this photograph is the honour of the clock   clunk
that's terrible english   !ferret!   *(ding)* western star which breeds it
s too jarred for words   (cough)   and so between the hunk
        (cough)   whom we must admire and the slow persistent trees
(like instructions ||: to repeat a theme, the rock of aegis squashed our trunk)
overhanging the Federation-style avenue :|| our retinas
will not be torn by harshest ultraviolet light Our dinners
are rich and well attended we send emails with ease
even from remote snowy places to soar from history
shadows and ghosts and flames in the backblocks of our eyes
cranberries becoming blueberries in the frost:
well the mist in your gaze (correction: *hulk)* our gazes miss
and then they find each other somewhere else
(than this?) as if it's occurred human and not too flawed
we (two lovers) are the wildest music of our time
as we head along the boulevard and are not lost

4. Waters

after Michel Deguy

La Seine était verte
in your arms a bunch of lilies
when I was born
musical space was born unhealed

the one I can't escape
hard to be convinced of, but when
the rest of the sound…
you could call it my own…

On my way to speak
another death
(it's a very large forest)
a powerful voice arose:

in the street's repertory
someone falls
and then indeed the rain
makes the Seine green in your arms

5. Cardiogram (May)

after Michel Deguy

The Seine was green on your arm
Further than the Pont Mirabeau under
the hillsides like a breath
The suburb valued us
I'd have wanted I'd
so need that you think well
But now the heart'
s courage like an outraged prisoner like a heart
will hunt self-remorse from the poem!
The lengthening day has deprived us of light
Night's ebb-tide detours the nights away from us
o my paradoxical love! we were starving ourselves of poetry
but the brave thing will be to starve the poem
of nothing's flavour over the taste of everything

6. Rue Cuvier

The fat guy's body language is sprawl and aggro.
He keeps prodding the younger well-dressed guy
on Harvard and Obama. It's all slightly mad.
In the middle, a friend beams like a TV anchor.
Three New York intellectuals are having their say,
body language and voices taking over the place –
hard not to think they're contemptuous of us
and themselves. They speak loudly, like theatre.
The cool French barman can't cope with it,
though he knows, no doubt, they'll pay. Then
the wives appear, one with a baby – suddenly, yes,
they're all packing up to go. The chicks argue
with the guys – but who is whose exactly?
No-one gets on. They're academics? journos?

　　　　　　　　　It doesn't matter.
Outside in the street, diamond rain is falling,
bulging the café's canopy then slopping down
like a wad of light gashed across the space.
The depth and slant of it transform rue Cuvier.
Once I carried a goldfish home in a plastic bag
half-filled with water – I was a child, eight or so, and
every fragile curve and lump of water entered me
as if water and fish were the very tissue of my flesh.
Children stare at what they carry. I feared the polythene,
splitting, would smash the fish's world. Just like that,
this swelling rain first builds, then splashes to the ground:
for a second it's the falling air a fish could breathe.
But this shower's beauty is, also, suddenness. It came
with a gust of cool as I turned the corner
and no less suddenly I ran here, seeing a table
in a bar. Then of course, the Americans,
the barman, what to order. And all the time,
wetness glistening the debris of fallen leaves,

rain plucking its strings while it turns traffic-roar
into whispers and hisses: now the crossing's stripes
smear whiteness through the cobbles' varnish. Watching this
could be like heaven. Watching time float,
as if it balances every way while things which move
seem to move nowhere. The New Yorkers are as boring
as New Yorkers can be: "Obama?" "You can't be serious."
"You could *work* for Condy." "Yeah, sure!" The phrases
mean nothing and fill the air with irritation:
the shower sluices it, drifts it from another world.
For two seconds I'm free of all my thoughts
of how this would be perfect if you were here –
it's nearly perfect anyhow: 3.30 in summer wet.
What I'm balancing - nothing must ever be lost –
is the dream of being with you, of each together.
A brief downpour opens up a world called happiness
carrying the thought of you, the touch of you,
when, right now, its absence breaks my heart.

7. Winter Trees

So how oblivious do you
have to be
to the fragrant, noisy day,
to thin, voice-filled streets

and distant klaxons glancing
through the sun's blazing cube –
yes, the crowded day
and the day that soon will go –

when everyone's out
and we've been sleeping,
withdrawing and returning
to the flesh's range,

to the river winding round
the water meadows,
to the updraft of doves
like hats blown off-course

★

Sparse wintry trees
are masks over glimmer
which is creamy stucco glare
from afternoon's warm stone:

they build the mind a net
so that it can, clear-eyed, shepherd
rippling walls of time
down laden valleys, on outlined hills

Aubade

If an extremely blue, misty, angular winter early morning
left its traces, its minnows and shimmers, in your eyes
almost creating blindness in the night's dew-spattered end
and certainly patching up those palm–tree tops with far-off cumulus

if the man walking on the beach, the huge Russian dog galloping by him,
if even the Polish coin in your hand swept up from the sand's scallops
and the clicking noises of the oleander leaves like strips in a fly screen –
if all these would make sense suddenly (in a burst of light)

(in the white outflow of a breaking wave) (in a quick overjoyed
memory of you) then I would see clearly the whole future:
I'd be someone standing in a farm on a stony mountain side,
looking out to a valley of mown fields. I'd be in my fifth floor Paris
                                                    apartment,

looking down over a boulevard's brackish traffic. I'd know where I was,
know how I am. Angular winter light would have revealed not just your
                                                    beauty,
but my own immersion in it, even all my speechless delight:
the minnows, the shimmers, the play of threaded light, rapid shade,

would have become my innerness, my inner sense of you.
Already I cannot live without you, cannot accept such emptiness.
The blue misty winter light withdraws from the mirrored sea.
At last I've woken up with you, at last the night was dark with fire.

"Thoughts spoken out loud..."

Thoughts spoken out loud
breath impelled below in the tidal estuary, in the river

in crevice and crevasse both in delight and light
by love and longing   desire's invisible fibre

incomprehensible longing searching for words,
words turning out later to be the simplest thoughts:

there on the table, a bunch of yellow and gold bottlebrushes
leaning away from each other akimbo in a grey Japanese vase

yet so connected in curve, wedge, spray arching
spinning in the suddenly dipping time-fold —

There, as you look, time's felt as real and physical
overwhelming at the point it disappears

turning, as it does, into one of many times
fused in the regard of things

not unlike the point of breakthrough in
the struggle to love and to be loved

in which completeness and transparence   (lucid, woven strands)
blend and flow in words and acts

Afterwords

from Luis Cernuda

1. White Shadows

Delicate shadows, white ones, sleeping on the beach,
sleeping in love, in their universe's flower,
on a bed of sand, of chances over,
they know nothing of life's burning colour.

Kisses free-fall from their lips like
useless pearls into uncontrollable sea;
grey pearls or perhaps ashen stars
with vanished light climbing up the sky.

Under the night the silent world runs aground;
under the night those fixed, dead faces fade away.
Oh yes, white, so white, only those white shadows,
light too gives off shadows. But these ones are blue.

2. Let's Never Try to Love

That night the sea couldn't sleep.
Tired of counting, always counting so many waves,
it wanted to live further away,
where someone would recognise its bitter colour.

It said vague things in a sleepless voice,
boats softly tied together
on a backdrop of night,
or bodies always pale, in their clothes of forgetfulness
voyaging to nothing.

It was singing of storms, of thunders released
under skies of shadow,
like shadow itself,
like a shadow always
rancorous with a bird-like star.

Its voice tracking through lights, rain, cold,
arrived in cities built as tall as clouds,
Calm Sky, Colorado, Hell's Glacier,
all of them pure with snow or with stars fallen
into the earth's hands.

But the sea tired of expecting these cities.
From now on its lonely love was a vague pretext
for a smile years back
which nobody noticed.

And slowly it went back to sleep once again
where no-one
knows nothing about anyone.
Where the world ends.

Climates

1. The Price of Wind

In the age of catastrophes —
its dry creeks the length of decades —
the price of wind was on everyone's lips.
We farmed it like we were angels.

A lost sale was unspent energy
buffeting down the neighbour's paddock,
and the way it mimicked all the phrases
which human breath can play with.

This wind's word, its unplantable seed,
grows from despair and blindness —
the earth's despair, the eye's narrowness.
Nothing hovers in its invisibility.

When you drive down to check the dam,
the future's like that brief, shiny water.
Dark, pale cirrus is streaked in it.
Snake-necked turtles are laying eggs in the last green.

2. Traditional

Made in America, the old harmonica
travelled the world
once it had taken on in Germany –
it was "the waistcoat pocket orchestra".

★

Electric cars pioneer flood-prone Oregon,
with a torque faster than petrol.
Quickly the truth went to Mobile –
it could have gone anywhere back then.

★

So who counts the millions who flee
from a firestorm there in the desert?
Only poetry's beyond forgiveness –
who dares speak for the dead today?

★

Tunes shift meaning with an eye's twinkle.
Himmler's daughter thought he was a hero,
spent her life trying to clear his name. A drover,
playing his harmonica, once calmed night's cattle.

★

A drover playing his harmonica
haunts the night.   We've such nostalgias to fear:
cruel, blind hatreds disguised as love
against which victims accept no apologia.

3. Question from the Floor

The breaking dawn, the hinted rain, incessant weathers –
the small hope, the great hope, the great despair –
the girl asking from the auditorium "What can be done?",
the mismatch, the roads not taken, the blank stare
at what must seem like foolishness beyond all druthers,
fuelled by greed and a sheer ineptitude for thinking on
the future though we can see the species holocaust
(boneyards of organisms in an already ruined coliseum)
and sense oceanic weariness past the coast's green-zone
where you and I breathe easily in our cooled solarium,
being passive, intervening less and less in case we exhaust
even this simple spot of earth, suppressing, pushing down
what fractures thought and consciousness:
                              that split
between a plan more elegant than trees burgeoning
in pre-Settlement parkland, richer than acts of return,
wiser than a balance which knows its own burnt offering –
and in fact, a wreckage of everyday anxiety deep in the gut
knowing the world's renewable despite each paid-off politician.

Blue Wren Poem

The wind-form is the heat-format of the moment
in which air gets budged from over there
to the small spaces under the verandah's tin.

A flowering is the flowering of invisibility.
Spindrifts, tumbleweed, curlicues, stasis –
whose shapes are the shapes of a line drawn

between dust, evaporation, glare. A
wind-form is the format of heat. The space
is grimy with dust, webs, wood, oceans.

A small exhalation walks through, floats through,
like a ghost or a short, quick river
which has unfurled, disentangling itself,

out of the main vacancy of time,
out of the crowded emptiness on time's edge.
Nothing to be seen, everything to be felt.

The heat grows until suddenly it's even made
living more simple – the way to cluster in shadow,
the way to lie down, the way to turn on the air

or listen to music. There's no escaping it.
Like here, a house just hums with its ducts,
glass walls revealed as a weak barrier, porous

as soil or pastry, while the outside keeps bearing down.
Brilliant white pool furniture drowns on the pavers.
Outside, they say, is catastrophe. It's loaded with risk.

That said, of course, this isn't what this poem's about.
The allegory of pressure is just that, a dimension
which we don't need and which adds nothing.

There's no external, no space to float and move.
No replication can replace the therm. Try
the glumness which accompanies endurance:

nothing substitutes for the wind-curl, the web-drift.
There's a thin layer of protection in the shadow
half-printed by the tin.   If you look down, then,

there's a blue wren's enamel shine on the step –
speck of dabbed turquoise next to his drab bride –
as they peck and hop in the sheltered dust. Such

detail can be lost – bobbins, birds, refuge, storms –
when we can't hold out against the tide,
when radiance blurs the future. The dream blocked.

The rose petal's sheen dies on the whitewash.
The sand blows in around the narrow grave.
Any thought of harvest is an aberration.

By the River

Parked under trees
on the other side of the dusty area
where trailers often get abandoned a few days
by truckies who don't want to pick up far from the freeway
and, yes, there's a gap in the tree-cover
opening a view, blue and blank, across the escarpment
towards more tree-filled gulleys and ridges cramming out
westwards forever beyond this glimmering skylight –
that's where I've driven the car and its honeyed duco –
the light's amber sheath on its pale blue grey –
to get a sense of openness off-road and of where
the new routes, old roads and highways go
into backblocks, unformed crown land, sideshows,
areas half-settled, half-rich, half-nightmare,
into country without water apart from winter rain
and summer storms which once topped up dams
but now are rare ghosts from climates melted in the past –
in fact, the closest flowing water's so far away
it's hard to remember where –

so, here with the door open and the cicadas
buzzing thinner sprays than usual for summer
we could be out for a drive chatting, fixed on this or that,
something picked up and put away and then resumed
like you might with a memory or going back to a repair job
("yes, I'll get that two-stroke finally to work"),
questions re-encountered to shift direction
or perhaps to lose it, and then a breakthrough as startling
as the dry green slope with its apple gums, blackboys, succulent ground cover,
in the way it never loses faith with air's immensity
nor with its own crowded care for flowering and pollen.
Looked at, it asks where is it? What makes a zone –
borderless, no-place, jumbled – what makes it bring the flight
of nectar-sucking honey-eaters, seed-pickers, fossickers,
and the thousand pencil-lines of native bees and flies?

It's nothing. Tomorrow it's not here. (The light will have changed,
we won't recognise it or think it as a place.) Maybe we'd go on talking,
or perhaps not, and the slope's richness will, most likely,
drift through us, seizing attention. Really, there's nothing
to focus us, but so much to take in – so much already said,
just beneath saying, the other side of it.   All the events
seem to open up, offering themselves; while a balance quivers

mid-air and settles. A branch etched against all that sky.
It's the rip in the photo: white paper under the emulsion.
The line runs like a vein across bone, not quite buried,
a whisper of blue on forearms, wrist or breast. It's
the line of water which once filled a crevice, now televised
from Mars – a tidal basin edged with corroded rock.
It's a circuit of water doing its motion of out and return.
Two king parrots fly through at this point, splashing
their reds and greens landing upwards in higher breeze:
they'd dawdle there forever, sleek rustling things,
looking out at the horizon like me. They're in the ironbark —
one side's a white canopy, but the flowers can be pale pink too.
Hard to classify even if the names seem to connect
and the structure floats there unanchored. Underswell, pressure, pulse,
rhythmic chime and hum, colours glancing back creamed off
from black and white, a thought inhabiting a brew
of gum leaves in their dangled swatches, a nest of random stones,
some declivity in the sun-struck, sandy ground that's not yet decline –
an infinitude of timeliness in arrival and departure of
those moments between ourselves – you, me – :
even if really there's no future, only a kind of joyfulness – a depth –
neither of us seeing how it had been flowering, drawing lightness to it.

Watching How A Rain Front Stops

1

as it starts to do background
having been vertical drop down shutter-noise
leaf-quivering up to your neck in it soaking green
rainy earth-smoke and scarves upon boughs melting into air
melding into background of lost ridges beyond the paddocks
the air-wall of something not seen because you can't see it
last month's mirroring creek buried under mist with its blind flow between
                                                              ponds,
regrowth bush on the far side and old, fenced land this side –
an overarching, moist clearness starting to saturate with blue-grey

2

within pale immensity which has permeated
the way the last ten minutes' change has occurred –
even the way each molecule of time was like a
snappy, wet branch swept across shoulder, through hair,
as I stepped back onto the verandah –
transformation happening as if marble turns to flesh
new breath on wet skin
while the threatening cloud-weight, bulging
across the range, starts to give way

3

to glinting bicycle spokes of once again look-alike daybreak light
through flecks of leaves, a
sudden spaciousness in the seeming quietness
(brooding quietness) (unstifled breathing calm)
the house   two fruiting quince trees   the shining spaniel
the loam's glint, drenched brilliant grass
and hardly to be noticed, the insects' rasp and saw
re-charging across edges and slopes
in the corners, low down, yet everywhere in

4

inertia and stillness, stilledness, everything happening
it blues the blueness growing
so cleanly back of the mind we see things we don't see,
yet they're seen — a huge untraceable lightness
remembered as an opening upwards   away over there
burnt paper climbing in a chimney's updraught
granulated sky with the suddenly sun-drenched grey heron picked out in the
                                                     dam
— poster-paint grey wings, his neck "morning-after-a-snowstorm-in-
                                         Kosciuszko" whiteness —
flapping up in three, four, five alarmed strokes

White-Tailed Deer

The small thump from nowhere, someone turning
a piece of tin, a door's buffeting noise closing across the gulley,
a neighbour — what are they doing out there? — dropping a trailer or a drum
in a paddock where damp grass's been drying out these last twenty minutes
in a final sun cube whose shattered gleam just now has
flooded through sprays of half-grown bluegums
traced on the shed-wall —
                            it happens — where? —
closing in mid-air between two never identified twigs
six metres up, or caught behind a bird song (was it that?
or just some other sound) caught the thousandth time
from outside the kitchen door, magnified for a second or two
then forgotten just as many thousand times. Like the thump,
it's forgotten so intensely that we all hear it as an event
not really known as an event, one which shifts
the breath, the blood-surge, and how we see,
back into shape. For a moment you understand
startled ecstasy — it's a squawky wattlebird landing
(no, that's a dream half-merged with a memory)
or it's the elbow's jerk with which the car boot slams,
happenings which aren't noticed or which can't be,
how the shopping brought home brushes the passage wall,
how events change time's flow beneath perception.
Really, you've no idea what's going on. You hardly grab a thing.

Networked. Transformative. Yes, the world glimmers.
The flash lies in the grass, is something and is nothing.
The yellow-throated bird scrabbles in the rangy grevillea.
A great ocean withdraws into perspective over my shoulder,
in the shadows of untended trees. A hum overtakes the orchestra
and a striated sense of inevitable time surpasses each local thought.
It's as if you can be fearless — a second or two — about
what is inextricable in feeling and movement and mood.
A dance becomes a fight, bodies tangled, then a dance again.
The light goes down like a glittering dark boulder buried in the soil.
An aurora flares in the half-heard resonance around the thing —

the thump, the door closing, the click that passes you by —
while intangibility takes a serpent's shape of wind-brushed molecules.
And how will it end? this half-traced ecstasy at merely being here.
Could anything be heard other than the after mode
of how we got there, made it out? Suddenly you realise
you're hearing a night-time forest floor, a twig snapped —
not this last light with its thin, gold trees and ragged openness —
but a moment's hesitation one night in a foreign country:
I was in up-state New York, there was a house in the woods,
there was indoor light of a dinner party, good people, drinks.
I'd stepped outside to get a sense of things, their loitering depth.
Earlier I'd seen startled deer leap a stone wall tumbled into bracken.

Two-Part Variations

for Stuart Cooke

1.

The palm tree frond
flaps
a flag-like wave
across the dampness –

across the sky –

twice my height,
high above,
a deep green frond
paddling grey air. –

In the marina
a thousand wires
clink and jostle – rattled, jingling –

playing their forest of pulleys
as old-style radio masts
and angular semaphores:

I could live here
between the moisture and
that sound –

or in the moment
recalled just now
when I'd left the plane

and was walking
across shallow dusk-lit puddles

arriving at Nadi after
the afternoon downpour

★

The palm tree frond
swirls
its loose curlicue
across the sky –

its many fingers
stop the wind tearing it:
a lattice-work, an ocean,
a furtherance
all seep through.

A scent of diesel lifts
from glistening concrete

2.

Don't forget to hang on
to the arching green spire
of that wind-tossed stalk

in the forgotten verge, unmown,
next to pungent tarmac laid
on the approach road:

the grasses have shot up
in a couple of drizzly weeks,
spear grass, wallaby grass,

many too hard to identify –
perhaps that's red grass –
and the tangle, what is it?

The bending seed-head,
its shepherd's crook,
is about to ripen

and scatter invisible
golden particles into
undergrowth's rubbish

*

Follow along the inside
of the curve: there are tiny seeds
still about to ripen

on a trajectory more
certain than persistent weather
from the west over there

despite all its storms, rain-fronts,
even its monsoons pushed down
lower through the arid zone.

Mostly, the sheep ran off,
thousands of them,
long ago in childhood –

into sleep, through fences,
through wooden gates,
slats, stiles. Yet the fragrance's

not sheep. Have you ever
stopped in the desert mountains
of Southern California?

and, after a storm, have you smelt,
when walking off the road,
those sweet soaked gardens of creosote?

3.

Don't forget, too, Australia's native rose
there on its Dutch paper...
Delicate, not rose-like at all.

It has lasted a while,
Boronia serrulata,
watercolour by Raper,

flowering on a two-pronged
spray, picked somewhere
from sandstone rocks

circa 1790...Inked in its frame,
a long-dead instance trapped
in the particulars of blossom.

In the taxonomy of things,
a thing – but also no more
than a trace or capturing:

drawn from this order
to another one, observed
but thereby made border-

line, special for some people:
a diligent amateur's work
that's both cute and imperial.

A colonial picture, it snaps up
the land, the names, the space –
it plays its part in the game.

You look across the amber air
which is what is left
glowing around the flower,

immersed in its silence,
its wordlessness, its muteness,
its precision in the dance.

★

Wake up, wake up! Daybreak
down the beach,
past those sentinel outward-leaning coco-palms,

opens its white singular eye
over the grey waters
between clouds dark as berries

water-laden to the point of burst
but which will drift away
like a line of dolphins

now the warm atmosphere's
building to its later shine
of eye-strain white on dark.

So, wake up, let's go walking
through the water sluiced on sand,
tossing it from our feet like feathers:

watch out for things that sting.
The orange and lemon streaks
are in our blood.   The moisture's

what that blood must carry.
(The rose's pink and dark pink blushes)
The skin's permeable as the sand.

We're in the world, we have no choice
in how its transience is mine and yours.
Our shadowed gait's top-heavy as the palm.

Let's get there before the sun does.
We are in the world, we give it everything.
It hides itself, will soon be far too much.

Elegies

Orchard Bonfire

You've missed the tunnels of yellow mist
that effect of hillside cloud the wattles brew this year
and you've missed those graded bars of real cloud swelling up
in the west's intensest mixed-up light across the Brokenbacks
as early afternoon goes bright then nearly pours
you've missed that instant half-thought moment
where you recognise a bird-call or a frog –
one, a step of echoes, the other a chirr –
and the hysteric dog suddenly wound up ways away
through the trees on the neighbour's place
as I rake up leaves and debris to burn them
making a mountain out of gravity's falling tissue
you're missing how the low-down noise
of motorbikes (maybe a flock or flight of them)
arrives from the road through the valley
far off easily misheard a drone added to atmosphere
and how that sound is no less a bud
than the twig's pinkish spur indicating
its future burst weeks off –
the bikies power off into where? into what? –
they power off inside my ear my space
returning the whole business of tidying and preparing
and the exhaled columning of twisting drifts of smoke
and how the flame grows out of darkness
the narrowest thread leaping pirouetting
till it fills up everything like a complete sky
burning along a crater of unchained fire
swarming and disintegrating an unutterable nature
taking stuff apart so that a whole slope combusts
how there's no stopping it –
an irreclaimable, undeniable beauty –
black vermicular incline of twig and ash and flame's
sinuous beauty   jagged fire in dark
all this being what you had every day
you'd been chosen for all of this to have it to be it
I saw in you only such beauty

more even than its name
now what's left is grief past any sort of name
what's missed is more even than the whole day

April

The sunset's pink patches
trails happening through clouds
a slow dissolve
the last ray tilted
bursting out against the black
ridge with its silhouetted
stick-trees
picked out upon momentary
lemon – two or three seconds
of it –
where instantly a metal wall
stands out whitely
revealing the old shed
in a kind of hole between trees
never before noticed
a split second
reorganising
the world
anchoring it in
a single thought

no, a singular thought
of fade-out
in which energy slips
through the nerves' network
because it's like the end
unspeakable sadness
because it's the end
for weeks you were dying
(I can't bear it, even
to say it

The fire's wood smoke
drift through the branches
heat against the cold
that sudden sense of reversal
suddenly, more heat focussed
in a circle
yellow flames swarming
like a hand's palpitations
touching flesh massaging it
dangerous
beyond words
the slope is a whole incline
but the firebomb's
more intense at its heart
than any colour
beyond colour
how the heat takes over
as if the centre
must now fight against the
grains of darkness
which hang over cold, dry earth
glowing with them
and against them
covering the intensity
in a war with the rainbow
spectred
across the ridge
focussed on flames upshooting
from branches leaves twigs dust
holding heat together
converting them
in that skein
of fire
into immeasurables
and unknowns

Hundreds of K's Of It

...in warm wind which is now more sad than any words can say
in the wind which is like a slope of stained silk
in the wind bristling down the waves' blue terraces
in the wind which is inseparable from its own traced movement
in the wind which ducks under a wave
or leaps into it
pushing through an ice-cold hedge
in wind which has no choice other than to be alone
taking up the whole of space right to the edges
(lean against it, work against it)
in the wind which, choosing distance, is away over there
before it returns to touch in a hundred different ways
in the wind
in wind of white grains
grit sparking against arms and legs
in the wind with its diamond-head flutter
gliding over stone and the shadows of those passing
wind-snakes thick in the air
in warm wind utterly incapable yet bleating and blahing
— a squalling white blur —
in warm wind like spider-thread strung between horizons
in wind in this warm wind's intense light —
in wind which counts each moment bluffing and ticking
in wind which has been here long before me
wind like a glimpse of glittering, mirrored tidal waterway
the bordering trees reflected there in a darker smudge
in the wind
which as soon as it touches someone — me, him, her — has vanished
in the stillness of non-stop wind
the words we spoke already blown so
far away and unreclaimable
as if what they meant was just the mind's
arid country   hundreds of k's of it
for you will never be found again no matter
where and how this warm wind blows
no matter how

Cloud

Smaller than gnats, almost imperceptible, glistening flies
hovering in their edgeless clusters
shaping and reshaping sideways through winter sun's white light –
mid-air thrips emanating between shadow and light-ray –
thirty centimetres above damp long grass, matted weeds, cool earth,
visible and invisible as they swarm and float,
dots and instants one moment, noiseless aircraft the next,
homing for a place at sunset where they can land,
bubbling molecules escaping yet returning as flashes
on the eyes when staring at brightness: all of them exploding into an event
because they're seen or because, momentarily, they're intersected
by a slanted glare-effect which now races from the sandhill world
back here to temporary green depth — the flies coiling and startling
in soon-to-be-dusk air,
evidencing themselves as minuscules,
as splits, splinters, glints,
dots of grit between shadow and amber spandrel
tubed – no, framed – under branches of turpentines and apple gums
and in that way, quite possibly meaningless, quite possibly
microbes of non-significance suddenly there in the bare world's
sinking warmth:
                    microbes below significance as is any sense
of being that's brought into prominence when the context
seems lost, non-existent, a flicker darkening
in which (no less instantly) you remember details too terrible to
bring to mind of, say, a car crash or a house fire
(even of a murder or of a child drowned in the dam),
details a person will never fully remember, never accepting nor forgetting,
for they're details too tragic to narrate, too instant and cloudlike,
moment of shattering micro-second which your mind still scans:
thus, the 8 mins 19 secs which it takes this light-blip, this hillock
of incandescence, to arrive and settle measures a tranquillity
never to be borne – like the provocation of virtual particles dancing –
though it occurs every day in a glance, whether in grief, or even ecstasy.

Milk and Honey

1.

What would have been
the poem for you

has become an
overriding sense

of the day – taking it
for granted, as one does,

with its drives, its houses,
its office – all the

non-specifics by which
looking back, a

huge sunlit series
of changing moods

like grooved flat space
becomes a bare plain,

a wide riverless upland
under a lowering sky

which might be precipitation
threatened or passing over

or a storm building its
folding and unfolding

cabbage-leaves flung into
measureless altitude

in some dream
mountains. Cabbage, that is,

and acanthus. And
the mountains? Are they

mountains? Yes, the ones there...
The ones which ripple up

confused with cloudbands,
bulging across the skyline

like wadding or
insulation bats coming

loose in a roof. The
mountains are

both barrier and
points of escape, whether

going into them or over them,
offering their sublimes of

amethyst depth (sunset)
and exhilarating breath-

inhaling sunrise
salutations of

viewpoints (views where
we linger as if first light

will never shift, as if the
aquarium of specimens

will never empty, the ground
never be fully

exposed); or they're
the promise of a

country farther on, which
must be better, more

riverine, calm beyond
words or exclamation –

a "sea-change" valley
where black swans float

like silhouettes on
permanent silver water

overhung by paperbarks
whose boughs are

mirrored in shallow
translucences while

across the fence ginger-
toned cattle trundle

through deep grass, plantain,
burdock and reed clumps,

leaving overhead
a few inland pelicans

to anchor their
beaks and gullets

way across in the blue. Having
crossed the mountains,

there it is – beyond thought
and desire.   That said,

this is a day brimmed
with both those things –

impulses, wordless concepts –
too many thoughts to think

and aching desire and not just
mountains, frustrations,

plangent memory: all the
elements of the everyday

mind. I know no
moment free of them

once I have left
rare meditational calm

which is a brief, settled
state (how to stay there?)

even though, when in it,
I can hardly get up

to open or close a window
or switch on a fan and

it renders boiling an
egg an impossibility.

2.

Your poem is no egg.
Perhaps, though, it is

a smidgen or diminishing
imperceptible degree

closer to one than
any act of language

which somehow must
carry unbearably complex

feelings, intangible
depths of response and

an agreed way to think
and behave —

all out of order with
the intrinsic simplicity

(yes, I'm talking about
love again – really, yes –)

which shines through
every moment of

reflection on loss or joy.
Perhaps, rather, on their

memory where it would
be good to get the connector

between them: there would be
no drift, there would be

certainty in the system
and an adequate balance

of information: nightfall,
bird-twitter ceasing, the

rise of cicadas and frogs
like a border or fringe

holding an instant darker
world together, neither sad

nor ecstatic. Did the egg
hatch just now? did

ancientness and its im-
measurable swathe of time

allow the instant to drift
apart like the continents

are said to have done,
trapping each of us

in a few molecules swept
nowhere in surf, glitter, dust?

Good to be at one with them,
to bless them and be blessed.

3.

I work all day and in
the night – at last it's come,

cooler, not too heavy, almost
free of worry – I stay up to

add some words about the
stillnesss of a down-hanging

branch of flowering
lemon-scented gum –

it dangles over the
back verandah

beckoning gliders and
possums to their mutual

love of mouth and blossom,
nectar and shoot, their

leap, screech, squeal –
a pure ease with vacancy

out there beyond the
tree's glimmering net.

Across the gorge a shooting-
star goes down behind

the mostly patchy range whose
fires were months ago:

the star glitters a second,
two seconds, being debris

or satellite or some meteoric
flotsam, through leaves

and powdery flowers
outlined looming in the dark.

Alone, the poem's climbed that
rock-strewn, twig-charred slope

finding its well-watered land. It's
for the future. It feels.

Two For You

i.m. Nizar Bouheni

1. "As if I could get…"

---------- as if I could get
a handle on it

I never did

the half-seen,
        half-imagined

slant across space, ending
with a small

flitter –
        at first despair's

wing   becoming then

flight from the magnolia

flight from the apple bough

flight in the grass over the seed-heads

flight as a splice of
indicative warmth

well, I never got it
how to fling myself

through

★

the magistral bird

way up there
in an oceanic uplift

upwards-tending   "ever"

in the furnace

drawing up the horizon
around it -

immense like Australian sky
(I recall it so similar to

those drought years' sky – one year was
a rain-free eleven months)

   – the flickering dot drawn
in higher spirals –

paraclete to the pine-top
pinion to the pinnacle

launched up in the heat's
luminous sunset air

above the traffic murmur,
the roar, the voices,

the clutter of roofs,
walls, rooftop walks

★

As if I could get a
handle on its occurrence –

you were there, the bird
holding your attention

in a connection which
has now evaporated,

once part of a whole
world of dusk and air –

the white-roofed city in
its state of song

the landline's banded pink
reaching out

beyond the frontier

where sea meets land,
cloudless blue smirched

with petrol and dust
the two of us looking on

at, more or less, nothing
beyond the fact of it –

both of us hoping that
one day words and names

and the world's realness
would all line up

would just stay there

making it so apparent
that my memories of you

remain the clearest
thoughts of impulse, love, care

2. A Music

By now you've become
the perfect surfie

stepping across to the beach
through breaking waves

your board held on
your hip's left-side —

no right-side —
as you slip over those

hedges of light
bursting in flowers —

as you emerge and
disappear in the sun glare —

black skin gleaming
with water as if

you yourself alone
are a play of lightness

being darkness, able
to pad through sunbursts

and step out of clouds —
having gone so far out

in mood and sense of self
(will you return? will

that darkness consume you?)
treading back here to

the previous, joyous world
of living, of family, of

friends – back to me – into a
world which loses you

as you trip and seem
to stumble – show-off! –

in some ripple which
patterns the sand with

shelled wrinkles,
making a fool of

yourself, conscious and
unconscious of

standing there:
no photo. Just life.

★

Writing this – each poem –
will sum up tones of blue,

their shadow-play across
the water – green glass

with its own gull afloat
for five seconds,

splashing grey on white
to lift up across the air:

it'll enunciate each thing
while never making clear

how to speak into
the burial grounds

despite all the water's
darkness at its breast –

hypogées with hidden
access-steps, sharp white

pinnacles, scattered nameless
stones dappled with pencil-

pines or the engraved
slabs there in the missionary

cemetery by the water
near Rawene where once

 I scraped moss from a flat
stone I was half-sitting on,

revealing word
by word a

chiselled copperplate
of *"And is it all*

as nothing" and then as
I removed more lichens

"to ye that pass by" –
transience on transience –

celebrating those who shipwrecked
and drowned in that

remote colonial
Northland harbour. Or:

the blank sculpture at
the heart of Prague –

final Jewish burial yard which,
neither garden nor sculpture,

stretches out in a miniature
forest of triangular unmatched

stones leaning every way
like a toy-town alternative

and which shocked me
into stillness and grief –

I was in Prague to read
poems at a festival;

or the Keats grave which
I've written about, where you

step in "under Rome's
azure sky" (that's Shelley)

past the Aurelian walls
to shaded scent of

yew-trees and cypress,
intensity of youth

and sickness, the friends
there in neighbouring

small yards excerpted
from lost being and foreignness;

or if (as now) we walk up
the track of broken

stones and cinders,
catching our balance after

parking next to the village's
remnant olive orchard –

where even today – the new millennium! –
scarved village women

come out for the
October olives, thrashing

spreading grey trees with long
sticks and pruning hooks,

blankets and wicker
baskets spread on the ground –

it's a scene from all-time
and no-time –

here, this place, with its
white-washed concrete wall

along one side of
the hilltop and beneath it

the huddled, faithful
assembly sheltered in

praise-filled heavenly words
done carefully in black paint

on tombs packed in
across the incline

so that, if we go on
walking further,

we can look back together
out across a rainless slope

towards a sea-brow
of Mediterranean:

this is where you have chosen

if I turn south (I'm alone here,
you sleep and sleep)

I'd face towards
Lampedusa

and, if east, we'd sail
to Sicily and Agrigento

★

Variations on a
classic allow for

the partial disinte
gration of the thing

which has achieved
perfection in strength,

balance, movement,
vivacity of thought –

so we can write letters
on the tablets grooved

by downpours and lightning,
putting finger exercises

of melody onto sombre
pedalled chords –

a green pear about
to ripen into gold

and blushing
pale amber – in

a space more virtual
than TV –

held there forever
in the cloud,

being neither light
nor heavy

★

The last view of the sea
was today: multi-coloured

sea of anchored weed and
light sweeping its snow

in endlessly ending sun
across wave bars,

the shallow troughs
and dimples, the bulbousness

of what it is that pushes,
pulsing, forward in

the transmutation of wind
into curve and lift,

itself taken from aeons
of the earth spun out

into the heart of its own
explosion – still travelling,

still gathering on-
going glitter across windscreens

of cars parked by the dunes
and the flicker of wire

holding the posts
now half-drowned in sand,

although it seems – half-buried,
leaning forward, crooked –

84

they've a journey in mind
too and a destination

like my own traipsing
unsteady bare-footed

with striped beach-towel in this
desolateness and fringed

re-growth – marram, pigface,
stunted she-oaks – even

a solitary crow landed
on a dead black branch

which didn't make it,
noticing me; the multi-coloured

water adds its submerged rocks,
deep embedded wrack,

shuttlecocks of wind
flittering on grained lines

bright as rain-wet
tram-tracks reflecting

upwards to that sky –
that same sky –

immense as nothing
caught on a lip (a split)

an overhang, not jutting out
or shuddering back –

just there! The singleness
of each event in

its own swerve and
sharpness, drawing

attention and attentiveness
making it seem as if anyone

could just see, grasp it,
wait to understand

what no-one understands
as a dying's key condition

which I can't face, no-one
I know can – no-one has –

since it happens so ir-
reversibly (I hadn't

seen, I hadn't
noticed how the bobbin

of shadow fell in
the gutter, I hadn't

gathered *shadow*
or *sparrow* tumbled

in the rhyme's
leafless bush) –

its singleness is
that split moment

when you walk off,
no-one realising,

into a street with
corners and lights

heading home,
heading through all

rapids, broken
stones and pavements –

time's dead architecture
open to the air –

through the stucco,
rusted metal, sun-

baked gravels – a
singleness with no

answer (here, I
neither remember

nor forget you)
travelling again into

darkness never
to be accepted

★

The last view of
the sea is – well – just

what I've jotted down
"above": place-names,

shadows, stones,

swerves, tracks,
watered darkness,

the bird-swooped grass,
an ocean's she-oak,

fans, cars, screens,
dunes, how one

remembers cloud-
baguettes and bars,

pots of snapdragons
in blinding summer sun,

how to imagine things which
have and haven't been seen –

even the permanent stillness in my
life back here whenever I'd

finished calling you – that sense
we had the whole world

where we knew no boundaries
as there are no boundaries

round a varnished bowl
of apples – yes, they were "pears" just now –

set up against old wood
and rendered brick –

and the room's other side
glass doors to a terrace

with a storm-front backing
up behind the islands

in its curtain of
thickening amethyst

laced with darker
blotchy crepe –

the single gull remaining
on the beach

inside its
spot lit sand.

All said. All done.

The single stone,
the pinnacles

of briskly glaring
sun in parks, down

roads of outer ocean
on the earth-curve

where the lone swimmer
strikes out, flashing into

the spray of light,
now there, now gone

and then once more
visible, moving to the turn:

what leaps out now
is an image of you

(already the confusion
of photo and memory's

happening like sepia
recalled as colour)

as if you're still available
as real and mindful

as someone I talk to,
phone, sort things out with,

able never to forget –
just there, just here –

returning from the water's
edge shining in

its brightness
from which, later, we

walk away over the scalloped,
sun-brimmed sand

heading back past
a restaurant, a hotel entrance

there on the half-crumbled
esplanade, to where

a dinted yellow taxi waits
with the driver playing fusion

or the latest from Cairo
or Madrid – you seem indifferent to it –

and it will take us back
through the evening's

warm, polluted, people-dotted,
half-planned streets

to the centre's crowded cafés and
to ourselves and love

★

Dark sea – bare, windswept
sea – dark humped sea which

reaches up the coast the
whole length of bay –

surprise – flatness –
elephant clouds

At dawn short waves make
their exhalation

like a quick breath
collapsing on the beach –

a quick drawing in
of the breath –

as they fall over along
rows and small tumbles,

a finger of pale myosotis
splitting the horizon

which is blue daybreak
reaching white-hearted

towards Malta between
mauve fists, black broccoli

of daybreak clouds, a
handful of gulls

fluttering at the water-
mark, low warm wind

clinging to the sand.
Space, stillness, that hush

which is like a body
rising and falling when

in a long sleep. I turn over
and wake to see you

walking back from
the loo past the half-open

balcony window in
this first light's

darkness and
radiant space —

your silhouette
more eye-catching than

any such radiant dark
or any ocean smoothed with

daylight, your movement
more deft and fluent

than floating clouds or
even than the ever-changing

one-foot, then two-feet
fountain of gulls

when they land in a
heap of breezy feathers

while some in slow motion
take off after crowding

each other at the
line of foam

where the waves (dreamt
as if particles) sink through

Dry Grass

It's sort of raining —
in a way, it's raining in the night,
but this night's not the real night
with a belt of real rain splayed across it
but the kind of darkness
you feel in separation
from someone you really love
someone you can't see for months

This rain —
whose real version hasn't happened —
slants through the night
which is your mind's darkness
the always unthought part of thought
the space back of the eyes
through the ear's untraced edge

dry invisible downpour in the night
sparks of rain-like fire
spatters of rain like wind-blown embers
heavier rain — after a lightning strike — pouring fringes of lace
drumming its fists on the verandah roof
cool housed sense of being inside
watching the quivering air
latent rain imaginary cloudburst
impossible to reach to within me
a blocked curtain of water is shimmering

In a way it's always raining in this dark
while here (again I'm sleepless, frustrated with it)
October's inland arid country night
grazes over the dry, still, quiet land
and, in pain without you —
literally, breathing pain and absence —
I've woken up and go outside

to watch how the empty paddock slopes
stretch out
as if they're sleeping shadow-bodies
able to luxuriate, folded into each other, in the star-dotted cool
forgetful of yesterday's heat — the wall of it —
which was blistering down
on unsheltered clay, on the yellow-flowering
fireweed and the already dead blond grass

ACKNOWLEDGEMENTS

The author would like to thank the editors of the journals where the following poems first appeared:

White Flowers 2011, *Poetry Review*. Volume 101, No 4 (Winter)

Wallabies 2009, *Poetry Review* Volume 99, No 1 (Spring) and *The Best Australian Poems 2009,* ed. Robert Adamson, Melbourne, Black Inc.

Poem 2012, *The Weekend Australian,* 18–19 August

About Bats 2009, *Southerly* 69/3 and *The Best Australian Poems 2010,* ed. Robert Adamson, Melbourne, Black Inc.

Summer Rain Front, North Coast 2011, *Virginia Quarterly Review* (Summer)

Daybreak 2012, *The Weekend Australian,* 28–29 July

You Do All These Things For Me: 2009, *Southerly* 69/3

A Park 2010, *Perihelion: A Journal of Poetry* 19 (Winter 2010)

Waters *after Michel Deguy* 2010, *Southerly* 70:1

Cardiogram (May) *after Michel Deguy* 2010, *Southerly* 70:1

Aubade 2009, *Out of The Box: Contemporary Australian Gay and Lesbian Poets,* eds. Michael Farrell and Jill Jones, Sydney, Puncher and Wattman and *The Best Australian Poems 2010,* ed. Robert Adamson, Melbourne, Black Inc.

Patio 2012, *Meanjin* 71:2 (Winter)

The Price of Wind 2008, *Edinburgh Review,* "Belongin Place", 122

Blue Wren Poem 2013, *Living Things,* Sydney, Vagabond Press

By the River 2014, *Poem: International English Language Quarterly*

Watching How a Rain Front Stops 2013, *The Best Australian Poems,* ed. Lisa Gorton, Melbourne, Black Inc.

White-Tailed Deer 2013, *TEXT Journal* 17:2

Orchard Bonfire 2012, *Meanjin* 71:2 (Winter)

April 2011, *Poetry Review* Volume 101, No 4 (Winter)

Hundreds of K's Of It 2013, *Australian Love Poems,* ed. Mark Tredinnick, Melbourne, Inkerman and Blunt

Cloud 2013, *Poem: International English Language Quarterly*

Milk and Honey 2013, *Cordite Poetry Review* (December 2013), in "Proteaceae" ed. Peter Minter

Dry Grass 2008, *Edinburgh Review,* "Belongin Place", 122

NOTES ON THE POEMS

Luis Cernuda's Sombras Blancas and No Intentemos El Amor Nunca are from his 1929 collection *El Rio, El Amor*. Leaving Paris was first broadcast on ABC Radio National's *Poetica* (24 September 2011) and is available in a podcast program with a variety of other poems, A Ruined Building Filled with Voices: An Interview and Readings with Martin Harrison. The poem is made of responses to a randomly sorted set of instructions repeated four times which were then destroyed. Two For You is loosely based on the classical *nuba* form of traditional Tunisian Maloufi performance which combines both strict tempi and opportunities for extended improvisation for the singer and musicians. The majority of the later parts of a *nuba* performance are *qasidahs* or laments.

Martin Harrison

Martin Harrison's *Wild Bees: New and Selected Poems* is also published by University of Western Australia Publishing, first appearing in 2008. This volume *Happiness* selects from his poetry since then. His poems have been widely translated into Chinese, principally by Shaoyang Zhang and into French by Marilyne Bertoncini. As well as being the author of seven earlier books of poetry Martin Harrison widely published essays and criticism. Some of this writing appeared in *Who Wants to Create Australia* (Halstead Press 2004). Martin Harrison lived in the Hunter Valley, New South Wales, and taught writing and poetry at the University of Technology, Sydney. He died in 2014.

www.ingramcontent.com/pod-product-compliance
Lightning Source LLC
Chambersburg PA
CBHW031559040426
42452CB00006B/360

www.ingramcontent.com/pod-product-compliance
Lightning Source LLC
Chambersburg PA
CBHW031559040426